HURON ____ LIBRARY

MW00964114

3 6492 00519312 0

DISCARD

J 819.154 Page

Page, P.
A Brazilian alphabet for the
younger reader.

PRICE: $16.95 (3559/go   )

Books by P. K. Page

Poetry
As Ten as Twenty, 1946
The Metal and the Flower, 1954
Cry Ararat! Poems New and Selected, 1967
P. K. Page: Poems Selected and New, 1974
Evening Dance of the Grey Flies, 1981
The Glass Air, 1985, 1991
Hologram, 1994
The Hidden Room (in two volumes), 1997
And Once More Saw the Stars — Four Poems for Two Voices
      (with Philip Stratford), 2001
Planet Earth, 2002
Cosmologies, 2003

Poetry Anthology
To Say the Least: Canadian Poets from A to Z, 1979

Prose
The Sun and the Moon, 1944, 1973
Brazilian Journal, 1988
Unless the Eye Catch Fire, 1994
A Kind of Fiction, 2001

For Children
A Flask of Sea Water, 1989
The Travelling Musicians, 1991
The Goat That Flew, 1994
A Grain of Sand, 2003

P K PAGE

A **B**RAZILIAN ALPHABET FOR THE YOUNGER READER

The Porcupine's Quill

Library and Archives Canada Cataloguing in Publication

Page, P. K. (Patricia Kathleen), 1916–
   A Brazilian Alphabet for the Younger Reader/ by P. K. Page.

ISBN 0-88984-265-5

   1. Brazil–Juvenile literature. 2. Portuguese
language–Alphabet–Juvenile literature.   3. Alphabet books. I. Title.

F2508.5.P33 2005   j981   C2005-900797-4

Copyright © P.K. Page, 2005.
1 2 3 • 07 06 05

Published by The Porcupine's Quill (www.sentex.net/~pql)
68 Main Street, Erin, Ontario NOB ITO

Readied for the press by Tim Inkster; copy edited by Doris Cowan.
Typeset in Junius Modern, printed on Zephyr Antique laid,
and bound at the Porcupine's Quill Inc.

All rights reserved.
No reproduction without prior written permission of the publisher
except brief passages in reviews. Requests for photocopying or other
reprographic copying must be directed to Access Copyright.

Represented in Canada by the Literary Press Group.
Trade orders are available from the University of Toronto Press.

We acknowledge the support of the Ontario Arts Council,
and the Canada Council for the Arts for our publishing program.
The financial support of the Government of Canada through
the Book Publishing Industry Development Program is gratefully
acknowledged. Thanks, also, to the Government of Ontario through the
Ontario Media Development Corporation's Ontario Book Initiative.

Canada Council Conseil des Arts
for the Arts   du Canada

Canadä

ONTARIO ARTS COUNCIL
CONSEIL DES ARTS DE L'ONTARIO

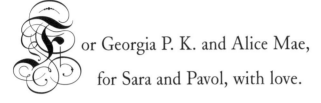or Georgia P. K. and Alice Mae,
for Sara and Pavol, with love.

BY WAY OF AN INTRODUCTION

Brazilian children, take note: your great great grandparents spelled this way. They lived before the spelling reform of 1931 — before double letters were eliminated, before Y became I or J, before K became Q or C, before — but that is all we need to know for this alphabet book. The old spellings match the nineteenth-century engravings and take us back in time.

When I was in Brazil and struggling to learn your language, I fell under the spell of your country — the greenness of the light falling through the palms, the sun and the sea — and under your spell, although you were not born yet, but I may have known your grandparents, and perhaps your parents when they were children. We may even have eaten *feijoada* together — your grandparents and I — or *vatapá* or delicious *doces*.

Brasilia, your new capital, was being built at the time, at the instigation of President Kubitschek. And when he was asked why the entrances to Niemeyer's government buildings were all underground, he replied, 'Meu Michelángelo tem alma de tatu.' (My Michelangelo has the soul of an armadillo). So I am especially glad to have a *tatu* in this alphabet. And splendid he is, as you will see when you reach the letter T, with his stone coat and his fine little feet.

I could not have imagined, then, that today I would be writing an A B C for those Canadian children who might like to learn a few foreign words — or for anyone at all who is prepared for a bit of nonsense mixed with old engravings — engravings that date back to your *great* or even your *great-great* grandparents' time. And little did I think I would be using your voice in which to do so. But we don't, as a rule, think so far ahead.

Try to imagine what you will be doing in fifty years' time. Going to the moon, maybe? Or ... *you* guess.

A is ARARA —
you call it macaw.
It has blue and gold feathers
and talks like your Pa.

B is BANANA.

You use the same word.

But it grows in *our* gardens.

Is that not absurd?

C is for CESTA —

a basket of flowers

all colours and sizes

in bunches and showers.

DONA DE CASA

means Mum of the house.

She'll kiss you and cure you

of ringworm and louse.

is ESCOLA.

You study at school

your letters and numbers

then swim in the pool.

F is FAZENDA —

a beautiful farm

where coffee beans ripen

when weather is warm.

is GALLINHA.
This hen wins the prize
for her feathery headdress.
But where are her eyes?

is for HOJE —

the word means today.

When Hoje is Saturday

then we can play.

I is for IRMÃ,

a girl's name to you.

To us it means sister.

Sis, how do you do!

JANELA — a window —

    it gives us our light —

but also it gives us

our darkness at night.

K is KAMICHI —

a monster who screams.

Don't tickle his horn

or he'll haunt you in dreams.

LIVRO is book,

and if you're a book lover

you'll know you can't tell

a good book by its cover.

MACACO is monkey.

We laugh when we see

that one looks like you

and the other like me!

NETO and NETA —

grandson and granddaughter.
The children of either
your son or your daughter.

OLHO is eye.

With the eyes in our head

we see blue and yellow

we see green and red.

PALMEIRAS are palm trees.
They grow up so high
you'd think they were trying
to reach for the sky.

Q's QUITANDEIRA.
She'll sell you a treat —
ripe mangoes and sugar cane
scrumptious and sweet!

R is for RIO —

a river, to you.

For us it's both river

and large city too.

SABIÁ is our robin.

He has a red breast

and sings and eats worms.

We love him the best.

TATU 's armadillo.

He has a bone coat

but the ants that he eats

surely tickle his throat.

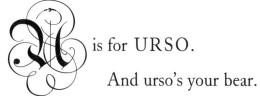 is for URSO.

And urso's your bear.

When you see him up north

does he give you a scare?

VACA is cow —

she's the source of ice cream

and butter and milk.

And she moos like a dream.

’s nothing.

    Believe it or not

it doesn't exist

in Brazil's alphabet.

X is XAROPE —

a syrup for wheezes

and all kinds of coughs.

It may even cure sneezes.

ETI's a monster

who lives in the snows.

Bigfoot, they call him.

Just look at his toes.

ZABUMBA — zabumba,
zabumba bum-bum!
I am sure you have guessed —
it's your very big drum.

A WORD FROM THE AUTHOR

The idea for this little book was first suggested at a party at Arlene Lampert's in the historic Distillery District of Toronto in September, 2004. Since then, many friends, and friends of friends, have had their many fingers in it — linguists, botanists, booksellers, diplomats, publishing interns and professors emeritus. Thanks to all, but thanks, especially, to my Brazilian friends Sigrid Renaux and Desiree Jung. To my Canadian friends Camilla Turner and Lalit Srivastava, and to Lalit's friend Bob Brooke. Thanks, as well, to Ivanise de Melo Maciel at the Brazilian embassy in Ottawa who recommended the linguistic services of Juliana Bahia. Thanks to Tracie Smith at the University of Victoria, and Don McLeod at the University of Toronto; to Anne Michaels in Toronto, David Stokes in Guelph, Manfred Meurer in Stratford, David Mason in Toronto and Jack Illingworth at the Porcupine's Quill in Erin Village.

A NOTE ON THE TEXT

Yeti is not a word that appears in Portuguese dictionaries, but it is a word that appears on 4,030 websites known to google (as of January 29, 2005) when the language tool option is set to Portuguese and the location to Brazil.

The modern Portuguese 'galinha' would have been spelled gallinha prior to the Spelling Reform adopted in Brazil in 1931. We use the old spelling here to match the nineteenth-century engravings that accompany the text.

The word kamichi does not appear in the authoritative *Diction'ario Aur'elio da Lingua Portuguesa*. The word does appear in the *Novo Dictionario da Lingua Portuguesa e Inglesa por H. Michaelis* (1945) which was in the author's possession when she arrived in Brazil in 1957.

There are no words in Portuguese that begin with the letter W.

BARBARA PEDRICK

P. K. Page spent over two years (1957–59) in Brazil while her husband, the late Arthur Irwin, served as Canadian ambassador stationed in Rio de Janeiro. Her vivid recollections of the tour, bracketed by ocean voyages embarking and disembarking in Manhattan, are collected in her *Brazilian Journal* (Lester & Orpen, Dennys, 1987). She has written several books for children, including *A Grain of Sand, The Goat That Flew, The Travelling Musicians,* and *A Flask of Sea Water.* Her selected poems, *Planet Earth*, appeared in 2002.

About her time in Brazil, Page has written: 'I find it hard now to remember why Brazil fell on my heart with so heavy a thud. Perhaps it was the memory of the Latin-American diplomatic wives in Ottawa who had looked like a cross between women and precious stones; perhaps an unformulated wish for a European post after Australia; perhaps ... who knows? At any rate I didn't view the prospect with particular cheer. Yet, curiously, all that I was loving about New Guinea — the marvellous fret of tropical vegetation, the moist, hot air, the extraordinary brilliance of bougainvillea and hibiscus against the rank and thrusting green — all of these were to be given to us even more abundantly in Brazil. All these and heaven too.' (*Brazilian Journal*)